PLANT-POWERED
K I T C H E N

51 DELICIOUS PLANT-BASED RECIPES

DR. AMANDA LEVITT

ALTERNATIVE
DAILY

CONTENTS

"Eat food. Not too much. Mostly plants."

Michael Pollan, In Defense of Food: An Eater's Manifesto

One of the most important pieces of health advice I give my patients about nutrition is this:

Eat a more plant-based diet!

You may have heard the term "plant-based" and envisioned eating a salad for every meal and never being able to enjoy a steak again. As a physician, I am a realist. I know that each small healthy behavioral change contributes to better health. I don't expect my patients who eat meat or chicken three times a day to stop "cold turkey" (pun intended). Moving toward a more plant-based diet simply means incorporating more whole, unprocessed foods that come from plants.

WHAT ABOUT PROTEIN?

It is a popular misconception that you can't get enough protein from a vegetarian diet. Not true. A plant-based diet can absolutely provide all of the essential amino acids (the building blocks of protein) that you need for optimal health. You do not need to worry about combining food types in order to get a balanced array of protein in each meal. In most instances, simply eating a wide variety of fresh fruits, vegetables, legumes, nuts, seeds, and whole grains will ensure that you get all the protein and nutrients you require. If you work out with weights or feel that you need supplementation, try a pea, hemp, or rice-based protein powder. If you follow a purely vegan diet (no animal products), you may need to supplement with vitamin B12 and vitamin D.

WHAT DOES PLANT-BASED MEAN?

A whole foods plant-based diet is centered on whole, unrefined, or minimally refined plants. It is a diet based on fruits, vegetables, tubers (root vegetables), nuts and seeds, whole grains, and legumes. It minimizes animal-based foods (including chicken, pork, beef, lamb and fish), dairy products, and eggs.

Plant-based doesn't mean you have to completely eliminate animal products. You can slowly find substitutes for animal protein by eating more beans/legumes/nuts and seeds, and try to use smaller amounts of high quality, grass-fed, organic animal products when you are consuming them.

As far as "whole food," the goal is also to reduce or eliminate highly processed foods like bleached, refined white flour, refined sugar, and to avoid artificial colors, flavors, hydrogenated and partially hydrogenated oils, high fructose corn syrup, and artificial sweeteners.

EXAMPLES OF PLANT-BASED, WHOLE FOODS INCLUDE:

- **Fruits:** mangos, bananas, grapes, strawberries, blueberries, raspberries, apples, pears, apricots, tangerines, peaches, oranges, cherries, blackberries, pineapple, kiwi etc.

- **Vegetables:** lettuce, collard greens, broccoli, cauliflower, kale, carrots, zucchini, mushrooms, onions, peppers, brussels sprouts, etc.

- **Tubers and starchy vegetables:** potatoes, sweet potatoes/yams, yucca, winter squash, corn

- **Whole grains:** millet, quinoa, barley, brown rice, whole wheat, farro, oats

- **Legumes:** kidney beans, chickpeas, lentils, lima beans, cannellini beans, black beans, fava beans, peanuts, soy (tofu, tempeh, edamame)

- **Nuts and seeds:** (walnuts, pecans, cashews, almonds, pistachios, Brazil nuts, sunflower seeds, pumpkin seeds, chia, flax, hemp)

"If it came from a plant, eat it; if it was made IN a plant, don't."

Michael Pollan

In addition to being healthier for the planet, a plant-based diet is healthier for you!

Plants are packed with phytonutrients including vitamins, minerals, antioxidants, polyphenols, anti-inflammatory agents, and anti-cancer compounds.

Numerous studies have found a strong correlation between a plant-based diet and longevity, immunity, improved mental health, and virtually every health measure you can think of. The science is clear: a plant-based diet is important for prevention of chronic diseases like heart disease, type 2 diabetes, cancer, and Alzheimer's, to name a few.

The American Academy of Nutrition and Dietetics and the American Diabetes Association both recommend a plant-based diet as being the most effective nutritional approach when it comes to managing blood glucose levels and preventing metabolic conditions such as diabetes.

The American Cancer Society also published a recommendation urging cancer survivors to eat a plant-based diet. The National Cancer Institute offered similar advice. The NCI contends that between 30 and 50 percent of cancers are diet-related, and that eating a variety of fresh fruits, vegetables, whole grains, and fiber-rich foods is the best way to ward off cancer.

Perhaps you have had a recent diagnosis and would like to make diet and lifestyle changes before starting medication. Or you might already be taking too many medications and are ready to take control of your health by making dietary changes. Or maybe you just want to lose weight and have more energy. These are all good reasons to start incorporating more plant foods into your diet.

One of the most powerful steps you can take to improve your health (and the health of our planet) is transition to a more plant-based diet. You don't have to be a strict vegan or vegetarian to reap the health benefits from eating a more plant-based whole foods diet and you don't have to sacrifice flavor!

HELPFUL TIPS:

Beans typically come dried or canned and can be easily added to or substituted for foods that you already eat. You can soak and cook your own dried beans, or simply stock canned beans on your pantry shelf for an inexpensive, convenient protein. When using canned beans, simply drain and rinse.

USEFUL CONVERSIONS FOR DRY VERSUS CANNED BEANS:

- 1 cup of dry beans yields approximately 3 cups of cooked beans

- A 15 ounce can = about 1 ½ cups of beans

- If a recipe calls for 1 cup of dried beans, you can use two 15-ounce cans.

- If a recipe calls for one 15-ounce can, you can cook ¾ cup of dried beans.

HOW TO COOK DRIED BEANS:

- Soak: 6-8 hours or overnight

- Cover beans with water by about 2 inches.

- Drain soaking water.

- Add fresh water (twice as much as dried beans). For example, if you have 1 cup of dried beans, add 2 cups of fresh water.

- For stovetop simmering: 45-60 minutes on a low heat.

- For pressure cooking: Bring heat up to high, allow pressure gauge to rise, then reduce heat (though still hot enough for the gauge to stay up) and cook for about 45 minutes.

- Salt AFTER cooking.

Beans are done when they are tender enough to mash easily in your mouth with your tongue.

HOW TO USE THIS RECIPE BOOK:

Most of the recipes in this cookbook are designed to accommodate food allergies, food sensitivity, and dietary restrictions.

In most recipes, you can easily substitute or interchange ingredients based on your personal dietary restrictions:

- Plant-based milks/sour cream/yogurt/cheese for dairy milk products
- Gluten free flour/oats for whole grain flour/oats
- Maple syrup for honey, if vegan

The recipes in this cookbook combine flavors from around the globe to delight your palate! Enjoy!

PLANT-POWERED OATMEAL WITH "THE WORKS"

This hearty vegan oatmeal uses oat milk or your favorite non-dairy milk to add a little extra protein. Get creative with your favorite fresh or frozen fruit and choice of nuts or seeds. One of my favorite combinations is raspberries and blueberries with shredded coconut, chopped pecans and a sprinkle of cinnamon on top!

TOTAL TIME: 10 minutes
SERVINGS: 2

INGREDIENTS

1 cup rolled oats

1 cup oat milk, almond milk, coconut milk or other non-dairy milk of your choice

1 cup water

½ teaspoon vanilla extract

½ teaspoon ground cinnamon

Fresh or frozen berries

Chopped walnuts, pecans, almonds, sunflower seeds, or pumpkin seeds

Ground flaxseeds

Unsweetened coconut flakes

1 tablespoon 100% maple syrup, optional

INSTRUCTIONS

1 Combine the oats, milk, water, vanilla, and cinnamon in a small pot. Bring to a boil over medium-high heat, then reduce to a gentle simmer. Cook, stirring occasionally, for a few minutes, until the oatmeal is soft and a little thinner than you'd like it. It will thicken quickly as it cools. If using frozen berries, add them while cooking.

2 To serve, divide the oatmeal between two bowls and top with fresh berries, nuts/seeds, and a sprinkling of flaxseed and coconut. Drizzle with maple syrup to taste, if desired.

EASY CHIA PUDDING
(WITH 5 DELICIOUS VARIATIONS)

Here is a base recipe for chia pudding, along with some of my favorite flavor variations, each of which can be prepared in under five minutes. Chia pudding is deliciously thick and creamy, with so many health benefits! It can be vegan, gluten free, raw, paleo, low calorie, low carb, and keto friendly… and you can eat chia pudding for a snack, for breakfast, or as a healthy dessert.

TOTAL TIME: 5 minutes
(plus at least 3-5 hours or overnight to thicken)
SERVINGS: 1-2

The key to a perfect chia pudding is to maintain the ratio of ¼ cup (4 tablespoons) of chia seeds to 1 cup of plant-based milk.

INGREDIENTS

1 cup plant-based milk (almond, coconut, soy, hemp, rice, cashew)

¼ cup chia seeds

¼ teaspoon pure vanilla extract

Sweetener of choice to taste (Sweetener amount will depend on the type of milk and sweetener you use. Options can include maple syrup, stevia, monk fruit extract, honey, or coconut sugar)

Scant ⅛ teaspoon salt

CHIA SEED PUDDING VARIATIONS:

Chocolate Fudge Chia Pudding: Add mini chocolate chips and 2 tablespoons cocoa powder or your favorite chocolate protein powder to the base recipe.

Strawberry Coconut: Use coconut milk for the milk of choice in the base recipe and garnish with sliced strawberries, or layer the pudding in a glass between layers of chopped berries.

Peanut Butter Cookie Dough: Stir 1-2 tablespoons peanut butter or powdered peanut butter into the base recipe.

INSTRUCTIONS

1 Whisk all ingredients in a container. Refrigerate in a covered container overnight (or at least for a minimum of 3-5 hours to thicken).

2 Once thickened, top with berries, cinnamon, coconut flakes, or toppings of your choice.

3 The pudding will keep 4-5 days refrigerated, so feel free to make a larger batch and portion into individual containers.

Chocolate Chip Banana Bread: Stir in mini chocolate chips and ¼ cup mashed banana.

Blueberry Pie Chia Pudding: Stir in ¼ cup mashed or pureed blueberries or blueberry yogurt. Top with fresh blueberries and a dash of cinnamon.

ENLIGHTENED SMOOTHIE BOWL

Smoothie bowls are popular for a reason. Why not start your day with a delicious, colorful bowl filled with nutritious fruit, protein, and fiber. This is a very forgiving recipe that you can adapt to your palate.

TOTAL TIME: 10 minutes
SERVINGS: 1

INGREDIENTS

SMOOTHIE MIX

1 ½ cups berry mix or frozen fruit mix of choice

1 ½ fresh banana
(use the other half sliced on top)

1-2 tablespoons almond or natural peanut butter or 1 scoop vegan protein powder, optional

½ cup water, coconut water, or plant-based milk (coconut, almond, rice, oat, soy)

3 – 4 ice cubes to desired thickness

Get creative with toppings... the combinations are endless!

OPTIONAL TOPPINGS:

Granola

Coconut

Cacao nibs

Natural nut butters
(almond, peanut, etc.)

Banana

Blueberries

Strawberries

Grapes

Kiwi

Goji berries

Hemp hearts

Chia seeds

Pomegranate seeds

Almonds

Pumpkin seeds

INSTRUCTIONS

1 In a blender, place berry mix, banana, nut butter, water, and ice cubes. Blend until thick and creamy.

2 Pour into a serving dish and top with whichever delicious toppings you like.

RECIPE NOTES:

- If using frozen bananas, omit the ice cubes and add approximately ¼ cup of water or plant-based milk as needed to achieve desired thickness.

- If adding protein powder, you may need to add a little extra water or plant-based milk as needed to achieve desired thickness.

- Topping with nuts and seeds will add extra protein.

TOASTED MUESLI WITH ALMONDS, COCONUT & DARK CHOCOLATE

Simple and delicious! Toasted muesli with almonds, coconut, and dark chocolate is a heart-healthy, homemade breakfast. Feel free to change up the mix-ins.

TOTAL TIME: 25 minutes
SERVINGS: 6-8

INGREDIENTS

MUESLI

4 cups old-fashioned oats

1 ½ cups sliced almonds

1 ½ cups large, unsweetened coconut flakes

Scant 1 teaspoon salt

½ teaspoon cinnamon

3 tablespoons maple syrup

2 tablespoons coconut oil, melted

2 teaspoons vanilla extract

½ cup mini dark dairy-free chocolate chips

SERVING SUGGESTIONS

Milk of choice (I like almond milk) or plain yogurt; dairy-free as desired

Sliced bananas, berries or fruit of choice

INSTRUCTIONS

1 Preheat oven to 350 F. For easy cleanup, line a large, rimmed baking sheet with parchment paper.

2 2. In a large mixing bowl, combine oats, almonds, coconut, salt, and cinnamon. Mix well. Pour in maple syrup, coconut oil, and vanilla extract and mix well. (Do NOT add chocolate chips; we're saving those for later.)

3 Pour mixture onto your baking sheet and bake until the oats and coconut flakes are lightly golden and fragrant, shaking the tray to mix halfway, about 15 minutes.

4 Let the muesli cool completely before mixing in the chocolate chips (if you add them too soon, the chips will melt).

5 Serve individual portions in bowls with almond milk or yogurt. For a chewier texture, let muesli rest for a few minutes so the oats soften up a bit. Enjoy!

6 Store cooled muesli in a freezer-safe bag with the air squeezed out. It keeps best in the freezer (no defrosting time required).

SWEET POTATO & BLACK BEAN BREAKFAST HASH

This is a "souped" up version of a breakfast hash. Sweet potatoes and black beans are a winning combination in this tasty vegan recipe. For non-vegan egg lovers: Top with 2 fried or poached free-range eggs.

TOTAL TIME: 40 minutes
SERVINGS: 4

INGREDIENTS

1 ¾ cups black bean soup, strained into a bowl to separate broth from beans

¼ cup water, or use strained broth from soup above

2 medium sweet potatoes, peeled and diced into small cubes

1 medium onion, diced

1 clove garlic, minced

2 cups kale, de-stemmed & finely chopped

½ teaspoon cumin

¼ teaspoon smoked paprika

½ teaspoon salt

TOP WITH:

¼ cup parsley or cilantro

½ avocado, sliced

Sprinkle of smoked paprika

INSTRUCTIONS

1 In a medium pan on medium heat, add in ¼ cup water (or ¼ cup strained broth), sweet potatoes, onions, and garlic.

2 Simmer covered, stirring occasionally, for 15 minutes. Add a little more water or broth if needed to avoid scorching.

3 Add kale and cumin and cook for another 15-20 minutes, or until the sweet potatoes are cooked and tender. Stir in the black beans reserved from the strained broth.

4 Salt and pepper to taste

5 Garnish with parsley or cilantro, avocado and smoked paprika. Top with eggs if desired. Serve warm.

BANANA SPLIT BOWL

Have a dessert-inspired morning with this vegan banana split breakfast bowl. Top with dairy-free yogurt, fresh berries, cacao nibs, and granola. Vegan, gluten-free and kid-friendly!

TOTAL TIME: 10 minutes
SERVINGS: 2

INGREDIENTS

2 bananas

Dash cinnamon

6 strawberries, sliced

¼ cup blueberries

2 5.3-ounce containers plain or vanilla almond or coconut milk yogurt (or substitute dairy yogurt if tolerated)

1 tablespoon cacao nibs

2 teaspoons smooth almond butter

100% maple syrup or honey

¼ cup granola (gluten free if needed)

INSTRUCTIONS

1 Peel bananas and cut each down the center with a knife.

2 Heat a skillet over medium heat and spray liberally with coconut oil cooking spray or use coconut oil melted in the pan. Add banana halves, split side down and let cook for 1-2 minutes, until the bottom is a little brown and the banana has softened a bit. Use a spatula to remove banana slices from the skillet, place on a plate to cool and sprinkle with a little cinnamon.

3 While bananas are cooling, wash berries and slice strawberries.

4 Arrange two banana halves in each bowl.

5 Add 1 container of yogurt into each bowl, allowing yogurt to cover most of the banana slices. Add fresh berries, cacao nibs and granola. Drizzle a little almond butter and maple syrup or honey over each and serve.

VARIATION:

For a busy morning, just use fresh bananas sliced in half without cooking, and top with yogurt, berries, maple syrup and almond butter.

HEALTHY BREAKFAST COOKIE

Cookies for breakfast? Yes! With wholesome ingredients like oats, almond meal, coconut, and peanut butter, you can feel good about eating this healthy breakfast cookie. Perfect for a grab-and-go option to power through your day!

TOTAL TIME: 30 minutes
SERVINGS: 12

INGREDIENTS

1 cup gluten-free rolled oats

½ cup almond meal

½ cup unsweetened shredded coconut

1 teaspoon ground cinnamon

½ teaspoon baking powder

½ teaspoon baking soda

½ teaspoon salt

2 chia eggs (instructions below)

¼ cup melted coconut oil

⅓ cup natural peanut butter (or almond butter)

⅓ cup pure maple syrup

1 teaspoon vanilla extract

¼ cup pumpkin seeds

¼ cup cranberries or raisins

¼ cup chopped walnut

¼ cup mini chocolate chips

INSTRUCTIONS

1 Preheat the oven to 350 F. Line a baking sheet with parchment paper and set aside.

2 To start, make the chia eggs. In a small bowl, whisk together 6 tablespoons of water with 2 tablespoons of chia seeds. Set aside for 10 minutes until the mixture becomes thick and gelatinous.

3 In a medium-sized bowl, combine oats, almond meal, shredded coconut, cinnamon, baking powder and soda, and salt.

4 In a small bowl, combine chia eggs, coconut oil, peanut butter, maple syrup, and vanilla extract. Add wet ingredients to dry and stir to combine.

5   Fold in pumpkin seeds, cranberries, walnuts, and chia seeds.

6   Round ¼ cup of dough into a ball and place on a baking sheet. Repeat until dough is gone. Press down lightly to form cookies and bake for 12-15 minutes until lightly browned.

7   Remove from the oven and let cookies cool for 10 minutes on a baking sheet before transferring them to a wire rack to cool completely.

8   Store in an airtight container for up to 5 days.

VEGAN SHEPHERD'S PIE

Shepherd's Pie is a classic comfort food. Traditional shepherd's pie contains ground beef, but this plant-based version is so flavorful and satisfying that you won't miss the meat! You will love this hearty, vegan shepherd's pie loaded with veggies and savory lentils, and of course, topped with fluffy mashed potatoes.

TOTAL TIME: 1 hour
SERVINGS: 6

INGREDIENTS

FILLING

1 medium onion, diced

2 cloves garlic, minced

1 ½ cups uncooked brown or green lentils, rinsed and drained

4 cups vegetable stock

2 teaspoons fresh thyme (or sub 1 teaspoon dried thyme per 2 teaspoons fresh)

One 10-ounce bag frozen mixed veggies: peas, carrots, green beans, and corn

MASHED POTATOES

3 pounds Yukon gold potatoes, partially peeled

3-4 tablespoons vegan butter (substitute regular butter if not vegan)

½ teaspoon garlic powder (optional)

Salt and pepper to taste

INSTRUCTIONS

1 Slice potatoes in half, place in a large pot and fill with water until they're just covered. Bring to a low boil on medium high heat, then generously salt, cover, and cook for 20-30 minutes or until tender. Once cooked, drain, add back to the pot to evaporate any remaining water, then transfer to a mixing bowl. Use a masher or large fork to mash until smooth. Add the desired amount of vegan butter, and season with salt and pepper to taste. Add garlic powder if desired. Loosely cover and set aside.

2 While potatoes are cooking, preheat oven to 425 F and lightly grease a 2-quart baking dish (or comparable sized dish, such as 9x13 pan).

3 In a large saucepan over medium heat, sauté onions and garlic in 1 tablespoon olive oil until lightly browned, about 5 minutes.

4 Add a pinch of salt and pepper. Then add lentils, stock, and thyme and stir. Bring to a low boil. Then reduce heat to simmer. Continue cooking until lentils are tender (35 to 40 minutes).

5 In the last 10 minutes of cooking, add the frozen veggies, stir to combine, and simmer covered.

6 OPTIONAL: To thicken the mixture, add 2 to 3 tablespoons mashed potatoes and stir. Alternatively, scoop out ½ of the mixture and whisk in 2 tablespoons cornstarch or arrowroot powder and whisk. Return to the pan and whisk to thicken.

7 Taste and adjust seasonings
   as needed. Then transfer
   to your prepared oven-safe
   baking dish and carefully
   top with mashed potatoes.
   Smooth down with a spoon
   or fork. Place on a baking
   sheet to catch overflow and
   bake for 10-15 minutes or
   until the mashed potatoes
   are lightly browned on top.

8 Let cool briefly before
   serving. The longer it sits,
   the more it will thicken.
   Cool completely before
   covering, and then store in
   the fridge for up to 4 days.
   Leftovers reheat nicely in the
   microwave for lunch.

HARISSA VEGGIE BOWL

Harissa is a spicy chili paste used in North African and Middle Eastern dishes. You can make your own, or simply pick up a prepared paste at most grocery stores. It packs a spicy kick that can elevate the flavor of almost any dish. This recipe makes ordinary vegetables taste extraordinary!

TOTAL TIME: 50 minutes
SERVINGS: 4 Bowls

INGREDIENTS

2 butternut squash peeled and cubed

4 red onions wedged

4 red bell peppers cut into strips

4 tablespoons harissa paste

4 tablespoons red wine vinegar

2 tablespoons olive oil

2 can garbanzo beans

2 teaspoons salt

2 teaspoons black pepper

2 teaspoons ground cumin

½ cup tahini

½ cup water

1 lemon, juiced

INSTRUCTIONS

1 Heat oven to 400 F.

2 Whisk together harissa paste, red wine vinegar, and olive oil in a small bowl. Drizzle mixture over butternut squash, onions, and peppers and stir to evenly coat.

3 Transfer vegetable mixture onto a parchment lined baking sheet and roast for 35 minutes.

4 While the vegetables are roasting, drain, rinse, and blot dry a can of garbanzo beans. Toss with salt, pepper, and cumin. Scatter beans over roasting vegetables during the last 20 minutes of cooking.

5 For tahini sauce: Whisk together tahini, water, and lemon juice.

6 Once vegetables are done roasting (butternut squash should be tender and easily pierced with a fork), serve over rice, kasha, couscous or other whole grain if desired.

7 Top with tahini dressing and enjoy!

CAULIFLOWER AND YELLOW LENTIL CURRY

This savory dish combines cauliflower and yellow lentils with red curry, ginger, garlic, turmeric, and curry powder. Plant-based, anti-inflammatory deliciousness! A dollop of mango jam or chutney rounds out the flavors and brings the dish to a whole new level!

TOTAL TIME: 1 hour
SERVINGS: 6

INGREDIENTS

1 onion, finely chopped

8 cloves garlic, minced

1–2 tablespoons fresh grated ginger

2 tablespoons oil

¼ cup curry paste (I used a red Thai curry paste)

½ teaspoon turmeric

½ teaspoon curry powder

3 cups vegetable broth + 3 cups water

2 cups dry yellow lentils or yellow split peas

1 or more heads cauliflower, chopped into bite sized pieces

Mango jam or chutney and chopped cilantro for serving

Salt to taste

INSTRUCTIONS

1   Sauté the onion, garlic, and ginger with the oil until soft, about 3 minutes. Add the curry paste, turmeric, and curry powder and stir fry for another 1 minute. Add the broth and water and whisk until combined. Bring to a boil.

2   Add the lentils and simmer for 20-40 minutes uncovered, stirring every so often. Add more water or broth as necessary. Yellow split peas will take longer to cook and, in my experience, they soak up more of the water, so you might need to add more water or broth.

3   When the lentils are almost done, add the cauliflower. Cover and simmer for 5-10 minutes or until cauliflower is tender-crisp. Stir to combine; season with salt to taste

4   Serve with mango chutney or jam and garnish with chopped cilantro.

BLACK BEAN TOSTADAS

A tostada is a crisp tortilla piled generously with any variety of toppings such as beans, salsa, and avocados. For an easy weeknight dinner, serve with a salad or steamed vegetable side. For company, this assemble-your-own tostada is a fun and festive dish!

TOTAL TIME: 30 minutes
SERVINGS: 8 tostadas, for 4 people

INGREDIENTS

8 corn tortillas

1 tablespoon extra-virgin olive oil

1 medium onion, finely chopped

2 to 4 cloves garlic, minced

Two (15-to 16-ounce) cans black beans, drained and rinsed, or 3 to 3½ cups cooked black beans

Juice of ½ lime to taste

1 to 2 small hot green chili peppers, seeded and sliced, optional

Salt and freshly ground pepper to taste

2 teaspoons ground cumin

GARNISHES

Shredded lettuce, baby greens, or baby spinach

Chunky salsa

Store-bought or homemade vegan sour cream or substitute dairy sour cream

Sliced ripe avocado or guacamole

INSTRUCTIONS

1 To toast the tortillas in the oven: Preheat the oven to 375 F. Spread the tortillas on a baking sheet. Bake for 10 minutes, or until crisp and dry and just starting to show a golden brown color in spots. Remove them from the oven and place them on a serving platter.

2 To toast the tortillas on a stovetop: Heat a large skillet. Toast the tortillas over medium heat (two or three at a time, depending on the size of the skillet) for about 5 minutes or so on each side, until crisp and touched with golden brown spots. Don't be afraid to let them get nice and crisp

3 Heat the oil in medium skillet. Add the onion and garlic and sauté until golden, about 5 minutes.

4 Add beans, lime juice, chili peppers if using, salt, pepper and cumin to the onions. Add ¼ cup water and bring to a simmer. Using a potato masher, mash some of the beans to thicken the texture.

5 To assemble the tostadas: Place the shredded lettuce, sour cream, salsa, avocado or guacamole in separate serving bowls and let each person assemble their tostadas as follows: Crispy tortilla base, layer on the lettuce, black bean mixture, and then desired toppings like sour cream, salsa, avocado or guacamole.

SWEET POTATO, BLACK BEAN, SPINACH, AND PEPPER ENCHILADAS WITH CILANTRO AVOCADO CREAM SAUCE

Sweet potatoes and black beans are one of my favorite combinations. These vegan enchiladas are so flavorful, you won't even miss the cheese!

TOTAL TIME: 1 hour
YIELD: 4 Enchiladas

INGREDIENTS

ENCHILADAS

1 tablespoon extra-virgin olive oil

1 onion, chopped (~2 cups)

2 garlic cloves, minced

1 cup sweet potato, chopped

1 red bell pepper, chopped

2 handfuls spinach, chopped

1 can black beans (~2 cups), drained and rinsed

About 2 ½ cups enchilada sauce

1 tablespoon nutritional yeast (optional)

1 ½ teaspoons ground cumin

1-2 tablespoons fresh lime juice, to taste

½ teaspoon kosher salt, or to taste

½ teaspoon garlic powder

1 teaspoon chili powder

⅛ teaspoon smoked paprika

4 whole grain tortilla wraps (gluten free wraps or use double the amount of corn tortillas if needed)

Cilantro Avocado Cream Sauce, to top

Green onion & chopped cilantro, to garnish

CILANTRO AVOCADO CREAM SAUCE

1 ¼ cup ripe avocado, pitted and peeled

2 tablespoons water, or more as needed to thin out

2-3 tablespoons lime juice, to taste

1 teaspoon apple cider vinegar

1 cup packed fresh cilantro

1 teaspoon kosher salt, to taste

½ teaspoon garlic powder

¾ teaspoon ground cumin

Black pepper, to taste

Red pepper flakes or cayenne pepper, to taste

INSTRUCTIONS

CILANTRO AVOCADO CREAM SAUCE

1 In a food processor, pulse the avocado and water until creamy. Then add in the rest of the ingredients and process until smooth. Use immediately for best results.

ENCHILADAS

1 Preheat oven to 350 F and prepare a baking dish large enough for 4 enchiladas.

2 Pre-cook chopped sweet potato by simmering it in a small pot of water for about 5-10 minutes until just fork tender. Do not overcook. Drain and set aside.

3 In a large skillet or pot, add 1 tablespoon of oil and bring to medium heat. Add in the chopped onion and cook for about 5 minutes, stirring often, until translucent. Add in garlic and reduce heat to low and cook for 2-3 more minutes. Next, add the chopped pepper, pre-cooked sweet potato, drained black beans, and chopped spinach. Cook for about 5-7 minutes on medium-low heat.

4 Add enchilada sauce. Stir well, and add in your seasonings: nutritional yeast (optional), cumin, fresh lime juice, salt, garlic powder, chili powder, smoked paprika- to taste. Adjust seasonings if necessary. Stir well.

5 To assemble enchiladas: Scoop about ¾ to 1 cup of the mixture onto the bottom of your casserole dish and spread out in a thin layer. Scoop about ½ to ¾ cup of the mixture onto each tortilla and wrap, placing the fold down on the casserole dish. Repeat for the remaining 3 tortillas and leave a bit of filling left to spread over the top.

6 Bake at 350 F for 18-20 minutes.

7 While enchiladas are baking, make the Cilantro Avocado Cream Sauce

8 When enchiladas are cooked, remove from the oven and pour cilantro cream sauce over top. Garnish with chopped cilantro and green onion. Serve immediately.

HEARTY WHITE BEAN AND KALE SOUP

This hearty soup combines white beans and greens in a thick, savory broth. It reheats well for a healthy lunch and you can even make an extra batch to freeze for another day!

TOTAL TIME: 55 minutes
SERVINGS: 4-6

INGREDIENTS

1 tablespoon extra-virgin olive oil

1 medium onion, chopped

1 large carrot, chopped

1 stick celery, chopped

Salt to taste

2 large garlic cloves, minced

1 (14-ounce) can chopped tomatoes, with juice

6 cups water or vegetable broth

1 tablespoon tomato paste

1 teaspoon oregano

1 medium Yukon gold potato (about 6 ounces), diced

Bay leaf, few sprigs of parsley, and thyme.

½ pound kale, stemmed, washed thoroughly, and chopped (4 cups chopped)

1 (15 ounce) can white beans, drained and rinsed

Freshly ground pepper

Grated parmesan for serving, optional

INSTRUCTIONS

1 Heat the olive oil over medium heat in a large, heavy soup pot and add the onions, carrots, and celery and a pinch of salt. Cook, stirring often, until vegetables are tender, about 8 minutes. Add garlic and cook, stirring, until fragrant, about 30 seconds. Stir in the tomatoes and juice from the can, add another pinch of salt and cook, stirring often, for 5 to 10 minutes, until the tomatoes have cooked down slightly.

2 Add water or broth, tomato paste, oregano, potato, and salt to taste. Bring to a boil, add bay leaf, parsley, and thyme, cover, and simmer 10 to 15 minutes, until potatoes are just about tender.

3 Add the kale and simmer for another 10 minutes until the kale and potatoes are tender. Taste, adjust salt, and add pepper. Stir in beans and simmer for 5 minutes.

4 Garnish each bowl with parmesan if desired.

CAJUN CAULIFLOWER BOWL

Cajun spice and lime makes this veggie bowl recipe pop with flavor! You will love the combination of fragrant basmati rice, crisp green beans, and roasted cauliflower. Topped with a tahini lime drizzle and scallions, this dish is sure to become a spice lover's favorite!

TOTAL TIME: 40 minutes
SERVINGS: 3 bowls

INGREDIENTS

1 ½ cups white basmati rice

2 ¼ cups water

½ teaspoon fine salt

12 ounces fresh green beans

CAULIFLOWER

1 pound fresh cauliflower florets

1 tablespoon Cajun seasoning (if using one with added salt, then omit the salt listed below)

2 teaspoons coconut sugar or maple syrup to taste

1 tablespoon lime juice

1 tablespoon water

½ teaspoon salt (omit if your Cajun seasoning has salt)

LIME TAHINI SAUCE

¼ cup tahini

¼ cup fresh lime juice

4 teaspoons water

2 teaspoons coconut sugar or maple syrup

¼ teaspoon salt

½ cup scallions, thinly sliced, optional for garnish

INSTRUCTIONS

1 Preheat the oven to 415 F and line 2 sheet pans with parchment paper. Set aside.

2 Add the rice, 2 ¼ cups water and ½ teaspoon salt to a medium pot and stir well. Bring to a boil over high heat and once boiling, stir once more, and cover with a lid. Turn down to the lowest heat and simmer for 15 minutes until all the water is evaporated. Remove from the heat and keep covered for 10 minutes only. This will steam the rice to finish cooking and yield perfect fluffy rice. Fluff with a fork and leave uncovered.

3 While the rice is cooking, prepare the cauliflower. In a large bowl, add Cajun seasoning, coconut sugar, salt, lime juice, and water and whisk well.

4 Add the cauliflower florets to the Cajun seasoning mixture, mixing well to be sure each floret is coated evenly with the seasoning.

5 Spread the cauliflower out evenly on the lined pan. Bake for 20 minutes until tender and cooked through. Shake pan, and switch to broil for 3-5 minutes for final browning and texture. Watch closely to avoid burning.

6 Add the green beans to the other lined pan, season with salt and pepper and a drizzle of olive oil, and place on the rack beneath the cauliflower at the same time. Cook 15-20 minutes or until desired tenderness.

7 While the veggies are baking, make the lime tahini sauce by adding tahini, lime juice, water, coconut sugar, and salt to a small bowl and whisk until smooth.

8 To serve, add a portion of rice to each bowl and add a portion of cauliflower and green beans. Garnish with a drizzle of lime tahini sauce and sprinkle with green onions on top.

THE BEST KALE CAESAR SALAD

If you love Caesar salad but need to avoid dairy and gluten, this colorful kale Caesar is a superfood delight! Roasted sweet potatoes, sweet dried cranberries, creamy avocado, protein packed chickpeas and tangy tahini Caesar dressing make this salad a satisfying nutrient-packed lunch or dinner.

TOTAL TIME: 60 minutes
SERVINGS: 4-6

INGREDIENTS

1 large sweet potato,
peeled and diced

5–6 cloves garlic, not peeled

1 large bunch curly kale,
stem removed and chopped

1 (15 ounce) can chickpeas,
drained and rinsed

½ small red onion, diced

⅓ cup dried cranberries

1 medium avocado,
sliced or cubed

Olive oil

Salt and pepper

Top with croutons- optional

TAHINI CESAR DRESSING:

½ cup tahini

Juice of 1 lemon

½ cup water

¼ teaspoon salt

Roasted garlic from above

INSTRUCTIONS

1 Preheat oven to 375 F.

2 On a large baking sheet, arrange the diced sweet potato in a single layer and the unpeeled garlic cloves off to one side. Drizzle potatoes and garlic with olive oil and season with salt and pepper.

3 Bake for about 40 minutes, until the sweet potatoes are tender and golden brown on the edges. Remove from the oven and set aside.

4 To make the dressing, remove the roasted garlic from the papery outer shell and place in a blender along with the tahini, water, lemon juice and salt. Blend for about 1 minute until creamy.

5 Place the chopped kale into a large bowl and squeeze a little bit of lemon juice over it and a sprinkle of salt. Use your hands to gently massage the leaves for about 30 seconds.

6 Pour about half of the dressing over the kale and use a spoon to mix until all the kale is coated with dressing. Top with roasted sweet potatoes, dried cranberries, chickpeas, onions and avocado and then drizzle the remaining dressing over top. Enjoy!

ONE-POT TUSCAN WHITE BEAN STEW WITH CHICKPEA PASTA

Chickpea pasta — which you can find in most grocery stores or online — is gluten-free and often packs at least double the protein and fiber as traditional pasta. Feel free to substitute any type of whole grain or gluten-free pasta.

TOTAL TIME: 18 minutes
SERVINGS: Serves 4
SERVING SIZE: About 2 cups

INGREDIENTS

¼ cup extra virgin olive oil

4 garlic cloves, thinly sliced

¼ teaspoon red pepper flakes

1 can (14.5 ounces) diced tomatoes

4 cups low-sodium vegetable broth

1 teaspoon kosher salt

½ teaspoon ground black pepper

1 cup dried chickpea pasta, shells, or any other whole grain pasta

1 can (15 ounces) white beans, drained

1 bunch Lacinato kale, stems removed, roughly chopped

Toasted bread and shaved parmesan to serve, optional

INSTRUCTIONS

1 Heat olive oil in a large pot over medium heat.

2 Add garlic and red pepper flakes and cook until fragrant, about 2 minutes.

3 Add diced tomatoes (with juices) and continue cooking for an additional 2 minutes.

4 Add vegetable broth, salt, pepper, and pasta.

5 Bring to a simmer and cook until pasta is tender, about 10 minutes.

6 Add white beans and kale and stir to wilt.

7 Serve with toasted bread and garnish with parmesan cheese-optional.

COCONUT CURRY CHICKPEAS WITH GREENS

This simple coconut curry is rich and flavorful. Baby kale or tender collards can be substituted for spinach if desired. Delicious served over a cooked grain like rice or quinoa.

TOTAL TIME: 20 minutes
SERVINGS: 4 servings

INGREDIENTS

2 tablespoons olive oil

1 medium onion, diced

3 cloves garlic, minced

1 tablespoon yellow curry powder

¼ teaspoon crushed red pepper flakes (optional)

2 tablespoons fresh parsley, chopped

1 can full-fat coconut milk

1 can (15 ounces) chickpeas, drained and rinsed

1 tablespoon lemon juice

4 large handfuls baby spinach

Sea salt to taste

Black pepper to taste

INSTRUCTIONS

1 In a large pan on the stovetop, heat the olive oil over medium heat. Add the onions and sauté for 5 minutes. Add the garlic, curry powder and crushed red pepper flakes and cook for an additional 1-2 minutes. This will release the aromas in the spices.

2 Add parsley, coconut milk and chickpeas. Bring to a gentle simmer and cook for 10 minutes.

3 Add lemon juice and spinach and cook for 1-2 minutes or until the spinach leaves are lightly wilted.

4 Taste, season with salt and pepper and serve warm over rice or other whole grain if desired.

VEGAN NIÇOISE SALAD WITH CHICKPEA SALAD & LEMON MUSTARD DRESSING

Niçoise salad is traditionally made with tuna and eggs. For a vegan, plant-based option, try this tangy salad made with chickpeas and capers!

TOTAL TIME: 25 minutes
SERVINGS: 4

INGREDIENTS

SALAD

2 cups lettuce, washed
and chopped

½ pound French green beans,
trimmed

8-10 red potatoes, halved

2 Persian cucumbers, sliced

¼ cup pitted olives

⅛ cup capers

CHICKPEA SALAD

1 (15 ounce) can chickpeas,
rinsed and drained

¼ cup celery, finely chopped

1 ½ tablespoons vegan
mayonnaise

1 tablespoon Dijon mustard

1 tablespoon dill, chopped

Salt and pepper to taste

LEMON MUSTARD & HERB DRESSING

½ cup extra virgin olive oil

1 lemon, juiced

2 tablespoons Dijon mustard

2 tablespoons parsley, chopped

1 tablespoon dill, chopped

Salt and pepper to taste

INSTRUCTIONS

1 For the dressing, Whisk olive oil, lemon juice, mustard, parsley, dill, salt, and pepper together in a small bowl and set aside.

2 In a separate bowl, mash chickpeas with finely chopped celery, dill, mayo and mustard. Salt and pepper to taste.

3 Place potato halves in cold water and bring to boil. Cook for 15 minutes until tender.

4 Add trimmed green beans to a pan of boiling water and cook until the green beans are bright green and crisp tender, 2 to 3 minutes. Immediately transfer beans to ice bath for 5 minutes to preserve crisp texture.

5 Place washed, dried, and chopped lettuce on a serving plate or bowl.

6 Top with chickpea mixture, cooked potatoes, and cooked green beans. Drizzle with dressing and garnish with sliced cucumbers, olives, and capers.

CHICKPEA FRITTERS WITH GREEN CHILLI AND CUCUMBER SALAD

These lightly-spiced chickpea fritters served with a zesty cucumber salad are perfect for a tasty lunch!

TOTAL TIME: 30 minutes
SERVINGS: 4

INGREDIENTS

1 can chickpeas (15 ounces), drained and rinsed

1 cup all-purpose or gluten free flour

1 teaspoon ground turmeric

1 tablespoon mild curry powder

2 eggs, or egg substitute (For each egg, mix together 1 tablespoon ground flax seed with 3 tablespoons of warm water. Let the mixture stand for one minute before using)

¾ cup coconut water

3 scallions or spring onions, finely sliced

Fresh ginger, thumb-sized piece, peeled and finely grated

2 tablespoons lime juice

1 teaspoon rice vinegar

½ teaspoon sugar

2 tablespoons, plus 2 teaspoons vegetable oil

1½ teaspoon ground cumin seeds

½ cucumber, sliced thinly

¾ cup (200g) plain Greek or vegan yogurt

Handful mint leaves, chopped

1-2 green chilies, sliced, optional

INSTRUCTIONS

1   Roughly mash the chickpeas in a bowl, using a fork.

2   Add ½ of flour, turmeric, curry, and ½ teaspoon salt into a big bowl. Make a well in the center, then crack in the eggs (or egg substitute) and whisk together, gradually incorporating the remainder of the flour. Pour in ¼ of the coconut water while whisking, make sure the batter is still lump-free, then whisk in the remaining coconut water until the batter is perfectly smooth. Stir in the mashed chickpeas and spring onions.

3   Heat 1 tablespoon of oil in a non-stick frying pan. Add spoonfuls of batter and cook for 2-3 minutes on each side, flipping after bubbles appear on the surface. When golden and cooked through, remove from heat and keep warm in the oven while you cook the rest in batches. Add more oil as needed for each batch.

4   For the cucumber dressing: In a separate bowl, add finely grated ginger and lime. Whisk in vinegar, sugar, 2 teaspoons oil and ground cumin seeds. Drizzle over the sliced cucumber, gently toss to distribute the dressing evenly.

5   Serve fritters with cucumber salad and garnish with yogurt, mint, and slices of chili.

BUFFALO CHICKPEA TACOS

Do you crave the spicy "kick"
of buffalo sauce, but want a
plant-based option? These Buffalo
Chickpea Tacos are delicious, and
easy to make.

TOTAL TIME: 25 minutes
SERVINGS: 4

INGREDIENTS

FOR THE TACOS

⅓ cup hot sauce

3 tablespoons Sriracha sauce

2 tablespoons extra-virgin olive oil or melted non-dairy butter

1 teaspoon distilled white vinegar

2-2 ½ cups cooked chickpeas, drained and rinsed

1 ½ cups finely chopped celery or cucumber

1 teaspoon olive oil or vegetable oil

1 medium green bell pepper, thinly sliced

1 medium red bell pepper, thinly sliced

½ teaspoon salt, divided

8-10 tortillas or taco shells (use corn for gluten-free option)

2 cups baby spinach

CELERY RANCH SAUCE (MAKES 1 CUP)

1 cup raw cashews, soaked for 15 minutes and drained,

⅔ cup plain unsweetened non-dairy milk (rice, coconut, almond)

½ teaspoon salt

2 teaspoons extra-virgin olive oil

¼ teaspoon black pepper

1 teaspoon garlic powder

¾ teaspoon onion powder

1 - 2 tablespoons nutritional yeast

2 teaspoons apple cider vinegar or distilled white vinegar

½ teaspoon celery seeds

½ teaspoon dried parsley

½ teaspoon dried thyme

¼ teaspoon dried dill

2 teaspoons finely chopped fresh chives or 1 teaspoon dried chives (optional)

INSTRUCTIONS

1 Celery ranch sauce: In a blender, combine the cashews, milk, salt, oil, pepper, garlic powder, onion powder, nutritional yeast, vinegar, parsley, thyme, and dill. Blend until smooth and creamy. Taste and adjust the seasonings. Add the chives (if using) and stir gently to combine.

2 Buffalo chickpeas: Combine the hot sauce, sriracha, olive oil, and vinegar in a medium bowl. Add the chickpeas, tossing to coat them in the sauce, and set aside.

3 In a separate medium bowl, toss celery with half of the celery ranch sauce. Save the remainder of the celery ranch sauce to drizzle over the top each taco (thin with a little water if needed).

4 Heat the oil in a large skillet over medium-high heat. Add the green bell pepper, red bell pepper, and ½ teaspoon of salt. Cook the peppers until they are starting to brown, 4 to 5 minutes, stirring occasionally.

5 Warm the tortillas before filling if desired.

6 To assemble the tacos: Add baby spinach, sautéed peppers, and celery to each taco. Add Buffalo chickpeas and top with a generous drizzle of the celery ranch sauce.

EASIEST BLACK BEAN BURGERS

Ready to upgrade your store-bought frozen veggie burgers? These home-made black bean burgers are packed with flavor and so simple to make in your food processor. Delicious topped with guacamole, lettuce, tomato and sliced red onion.

TOTAL TIME: 25 minutes
SERVINGS: 8

INGREDIENTS

½ cup raw walnuts

½ cup old-fashioned oats

2 cloves garlic, chopped

1 ½-inch knob fresh ginger, peeled and coarsely chopped

¼ cup onion, coarsely chopped

1 to 2 tablespoons pickled jalapeño slices

1 can black beans (15-ounce can or 1 ½ cups), drained and rinsed

¼ cup cilantro, coarsely chopped

½ teaspoon ground cumin

½ teaspoon dried oregano

½ teaspoon chipotle chili powder

½ teaspoon salt

¼ teaspoon black pepper, or more to taste

1 tablespoon ground flax seeds, or chia seeds

2 to 3 tablespoons dry breadcrumbs or flour (gluten-free if preferred)

INSTRUCTIONS

1 In a food processor, combine the walnuts, oats, garlic, ginger, onion, and jalapeños and pulse a few times, until the walnuts and onions are evenly chopped, 5 to 10 seconds. Add the beans, cilantro, cumin, oregano, chili powder, salt, pepper, and ground flax seed and process in 5-second intervals, until most of the beans break down. Do not puree—there should still be some whole beans for texture.

2 Transfer the mixture to a bowl. If the mixture is too wet, add breadcrumbs or flour and stir to combine.

3 Divide the mixture into 7 to 8 equal portions and shape into tightly packed patties.

4 Heat a large skillet over medium-high heat (add oil if desired). Place the patties in the skillet and cook for 4 to 6 minutes per side, or until golden brown. Alternatively, preheat the oven to 400 F. Place the patties on a medium baking sheet lined with parchment paper. Bake the burgers for 15 minutes, flip, and bake another 10 minutes, or until the burgers are golden.

5 Serve on a toasted whole grain bun with lettuce, tomato, sliced onions or guacamole or enjoy served over a salad.

JERK SWEET POTATO & BLACK BEAN CURRY

Jerk spice, ginger, and thyme make simple black beans and sweet potatoes burst with Caribbean flavor! Perfect served over rice or quinoa.

TOTAL TIME: 30 minutes
SERVINGS: 4

INGREDIENTS

2 onions, 1 diced, 1 roughly chopped

2 tablespoons olive oil

Thumb-size piece of ginger root, roughly chopped

1 small bunch cilantro, leaves and stalks separated

3 tablespoons jerk seasoning

2 thyme sprigs

1 (15 ounce) can chopped tomato

4 tablespoons red wine vinegar

3 tablespoons light brown sugar or 2 tablespoons of 100% maple syrup

2 vegetable stock cubes, crumbled

2 ½ cups water

2lbs (4-5 medium) sweet potato, peeled and cut into chunks

2 (15 ounce) cans black beans, rinsed and drained

Jar of marinated roasted red pepper, cut into thick slices

INSTRUCTIONS

1 Gently sauté the diced onion in the olive oil in a large frying pan.

2 Meanwhile, blend the roughly chopped onion, ginger, cilantro stalks, and jerk seasoning with a hand-held blender. Add to the softened onion, stirring occasionally, cooking until fragrant. Stir in the thyme, chopped tomatoes, vinegar, sugar (or maple syrup), and stock cubes with 2 ½ cups water and bring to a simmer for 10 minutes.

3 Add sweet potatoes and simmer for 10 more minutes. Stir in beans and peppers and simmer for another 5 minutes until the potatoes are tender. Adjust seasoning and add salt and pepper to taste.

4 Serve over rice with a garnish of cilantro leaves.

BURRITO BOWL WITH CHIPOTLE BLACK BEANS

Who doesn't love a healthy burrito bowl with veggies and greens? If you have leftover rice, this tasty dish can be ready in just 15 minutes. That's my kind of fast food!

TOTAL TIME: 15 minutes (if rice already cooked)
SERVINGS: 2 bowls

INGREDIENTS

1 cup basmati rice, cooked

1 tablespoons olive oil

2 garlic cloves, chopped

1 can black beans (15 ounce), drained and rinsed

1 tablespoon cider vinegar

1 teaspoon honey

1 tablespoon chipotle paste

1 large handful curly kale, chopped

1 avocado, halved and sliced

1 medium tomato, chopped

1 small red onion, chopped

FOR SERVING (OPTIONAL)

Chipotle hot sauce

Cilantro leaves

Lime wedges

INSTRUCTIONS

1 Cook the rice following pack instructions, and set aside.

2 In a medium saucepan, heat the oil, add the garlic, and cook for 2 minutes or until golden. Add the beans, vinegar, honey, and chipotle paste. Season with salt and pepper to taste.

3 Add kale and cover for 1-2 minutes until kale is tender.

4 Divide the rice between shallow bowls and top with beans, kale, avocado, tomato and onion. Serve with hot sauce, cilantro and lime wedges.

BLACK BEAN POTATO "NACHOS"

These addictive black bean nachos make a great veggie sharing dish for a party or movie night with crispy potatoes, a fresh red pepper salsa, and melty cheese.

TOTAL TIME: 30 minutes
SERVINGS: 3-4

INGREDIENTS

3 large potatoes cut into thin round slices

2 tablespoons olive oil

1 teaspoon smoked paprika

100g extra sharp cheddar, grated (or vegan cheese for dairy free)

1 can black beans, drained and rinsed

½ small pack cilantro, roughly chopped

FOR THE RED PEPPER SALSA:

1 tablespoon pickled jalapeños, chopped

2 tablespoons marinated roasted red peppers, chopped

1 tablespoon extra-virgin olive oil

1 small red onion, finely chopped

Salt and pepper to taste

INSTRUCTIONS

1 Heat oven to 375 F. Line two large baking sheets with baking parchment. Brush the potato slices with oil, then season with salt, pepper, and smoked paprika. Bake for 10-15 minutes until completely crisp. Shake tray midway to brown evenly.

2 Reduce oven to 325 F. Transfer half the crispy potatoes to an ovenproof dish, layer with half the beans and cheese, then repeat. Return to the oven for 5-10 minutes until the cheese melts.

3 Meanwhile, in a small bowl, combine all the salsa ingredients and season with salt and pepper to taste.

4 Serve nachos with salsa and garnish with cilantro.

BLACK BEAN
CHIMICHURRI SALAD

Chimichurri is a flavorful South American sauce that features parsley, cilantro and chilis. No more boring lunches! Spice up your lunchbox with this protein-rich black bean salad.

TOTAL TIME: 15 minutes
SERVINGS: 1 lunch bowl

INGREDIENTS

1 can black beans (15-ounce), drained and rinsed

1 tomato, roughly chopped

¼ red onion, roughly chopped

½ avocado, chopped

⅛ cup feta cheese, crumbled, optional

FOR THE CHIMICHURRI

1 large handful fresh cilantro

1 large handful fresh parsley

2 tablespoons red wine vinegar

2 tablespoons extra-virgin olive oil

½ garlic clove, roughly chopped

¼ teaspoon chili powder

¼ teaspoon ground cumin

INSTRUCTIONS

1 Blend chimichurri ingredients in a blender or food processor until combined. Season to taste with salt and pepper and set aside.

2 In a bowl or plastic container toss together beans, tomato, red onion, avocado, and feta, if using. Drizzle with chimichurri dressing before serving.

TUSCAN WHITE BEAN SKILLET WITH TOMATOES, MUSHROOMS, AND ARTICHOKES

This vegetarian skillet meal is made from pantry staples for a quick weeknight dinner!

TOTAL TIME: 30 minutes
SERVINGS: 4

INGREDIENTS

2 tablespoons extra-virgin olive oil, divided

8 ounces brown mushrooms, sliced

1 ½ cups diced yellow onions (about 1 large onion)

3 cloves garlic, minced

⅔ cup drained and chopped oil-packed sun dried tomatoes

2 (14.5-ounce) cans fire-roasted diced tomatoes

2 (14.5-ounce) cans drained and rinsed cannellini beans

14.5-ounce can quartered artichoke hearts, drained

½ teaspoon kosher salt

½ teaspoon black pepper

1 teaspoon dried oregano

½ teaspoon dried thyme

1 teaspoon sugar or honey

Parsley for garnish

INSTRUCTIONS

1   Heat one tablespoon of the oil in a 10-inch cast iron skillet set over medium-high heat. Working in batches, add the mushrooms to the pan in a single layer. Brown for 1 to 2 minutes per side; transfer to a bowl and repeat with remaining mushrooms.

2   Add the remaining tablespoon of oil to the pan; add the onions and sauté until lightly browned, about 3 minutes. Add garlic and sun-dried tomatoes and cook until fragrant and softened, another 2 minutes.

3   Add the diced tomatoes to the pan, along with the beans, artichoke hearts, salt, pepper, oregano, thyme, and sugar or honey. Cover the pan and turn heat down to medium. Let cook for about 10 minutes, until hot. Return the mushrooms to the pan and cook for another 1-2 minutes, until heated evenly.

4   Garnish with chopped parsley and serve with crusty bread (optional).

VEGETARIAN WHITE BEAN CHILI

Three kinds of beans add texture to this simple (and quick) white bean chili recipe. For a hearty dinner, serve with cornbread and a salad.

TOTAL TIME: 20 minutes
SERVINGS: 4

INGREDIENTS

2 teaspoons of olive oil

½ medium yellow onion, diced (about 1 cup)

1 teaspoon dried oregano

¼ teaspoon kosher salt + more to taste

⅛ teaspoon freshly ground black pepper + more to taste

3 medium cloves garlic, peeled and minced

2 teaspoons ground cumin

2 cups vegetable broth

1 (15-ounce) can cannellini beans, rinsed

1 (15-ounce) can navy beans, rinsed

1 (15-ounce) can chickpeas, rinsed

1 (4-ounce) can diced green chiles

¼ teaspoon ground cloves

⅛ - ¼ teaspoon ground (cayenne) red pepper (use less for less heat)

Juice of 1 medium lime

OPTIONAL TOPPINGS:

Fresh cilantro

Lime wedges to squeeze over the top

Sliced scallions

Diced onions

Grated cheese (cheddar or vegan cheese)

Diced avocado

Sour cream or vegan sour cream

A dash or two of green tabasco

INSTRUCTIONS

1   Set a medium-to-large pot over low heat. Add the olive oil, onion, oregano, ¼ teaspoon salt, and ⅛ teaspoon pepper. Cook the onion, stirring occasionally, until soft and translucent, about 8 minutes.

2   Add the garlic and cumin. Cook, stirring frequently, for another minute.

3   Add the broth, beans, chiles, cloves, and cayenne. Stir to combine. Increase heat to medium-high and bring to a boil. Reduce to a simmer and cook for 3-5 minutes.

4   Remove from heat. Run a potato masher or fork through 5-6 times just to smash a few of the beans to thicken texture.

5   To serve: Squeeze the lime over the top and stir. Adjust salt and pepper to taste, and add optional toppings if desired.

WHITE BEAN SHAKSHUKA

This white bean shakshuka is
a delicious vegan take on a
traditional Middle Eastern dish.

TOTAL TIME: 30 minutes
SERVINGS: 4

INGREDIENTS

2 tablespoons extra-virgin olive oil

1 yellow onion, finely chopped

3 cloves garlic, minced

1 head kale, with stems removed, chopped

28-ounce can diced or crushed tomatoes

2 teaspoons smoked paprika

1 teaspoon ground cumin

1 teaspoon dried oregano

½ teaspoon salt & pepper

Pinch of crushed red pepper (optional)

15-ounce can cannellini beans

Vegan cream cheese or yogurt, and a handful of chopped fresh parsley, for topping

INSTRUCTIONS

1 Warm olive oil in a large skillet over medium heat. Add the onions and cook until transparent. Add garlic and cook for a few more minutes, until fragrant. Then add the kale, cover, and cook for about 3 to 5 minutes, until the kale is wilted.

2 Add the tomatoes and their juices, smoked paprika, cumin, oregano, salt and pepper, and red pepper flakes (optional). Stir to combine and bring to a simmer. Add the white beans and cook until heated through. Remove from heat and set aside.

3 Top with dollops of vegan cream cheese and garnish with chopped parsley. Serve warm with toasted bread, and enjoy!

WHITE BEAN QUESADILLAS

These tasty, dairy-free quesadillas are filled with spicy white beans, creamy avocado slices, fresh tomatoes and fresh cilantro.

TOTAL TIME: 20 minutes
SERVINGS: 2

INGREDIENTS

1 (15-ounce) can cannellini beans, drained and rinsed

1 tablespoon hot sauce

½ teaspoon ground cumin

Salt and pepper to taste

2 medium (8-inch) flour tortillas or 3-4 corn tortillas

½ ripe avocado, sliced

¼ cup diced red onion (about ¼ of a medium onion)

¼ cup diced tomato (about 1 small Roma tomato)

2 tablespoons fresh cilantro, chopped

Olive oil

Salsa or additional hot sauce, for serving

INSTRUCTIONS

1 Place cannellini beans into a medium bowl and mash with a fork or potato masher, leaving the mixture as chunky as you like. Stir in hot sauce and cumin, then season with salt and pepper to taste.

2 Divide the bean mixture among tortillas, spreading in an even layer over each. Divide avocado slices over half of each tortilla, then sprinkle with tomato, onion, cilantro, and optionally a bit more hot sauce, salt, and pepper. Fold tortillas closed.

3 Lightly oil the bottom of a large skillet and place over medium heat. Arrange quesadillas in the skillet, and if your skillet has a lid, use it to cover them, as this will help the fillings get nice and warm. Cook until crisp and lightly browned on bottom, about 4 minutes. Gently flip and cook for about 4 minutes more, until browned on opposite sides.

4 Remove quesadillas from the skillet and slice, if desired. Serve with salsa, hot sauce, or your favorite quesadilla toppings.

CURRIED LENTIL, TOMATO, AND COCONUT SOUP

Coconut and curry spices combine to make a hearty, warming curry. Satisfying and delicious served over rice, quinoa, or other whole grain.

TOTAL TIME: 30 minutes
SERVINGS: 4

INGREDIENTS

2 tablespoons virgin coconut oil or extra-virgin olive oil

1 medium onion, finely chopped

2 garlic cloves, finely chopped

1 (2½ inch) piece ginger, peeled, finely grated

1 tablespoon curry powder

⅛ - ¼ teaspoon crushed red pepper flakes, adjust to taste

¾ cup red lentils

1 (14.5-ounce) can crushed tomatoes

½ cup finely chopped cilantro

Kosher salt and freshly ground pepper to taste

1 (13.5-ounce) can unsweetened coconut milk, shaken well, divided

Lime wedges (for serving)

INSTRUCTIONS

1 Heat oil in a medium saucepan over medium. Cook onion, stirring often, until softened and golden brown, 8–10 minutes.

2 Add garlic, ginger, curry powder, and red pepper flakes and cook, stirring, until fragrant, about 2 minutes.

3 Add lentils and cook, stirring, 1 minute. Add tomatoes, ½ cup cilantro, a generous pinch of salt, and 2½ cups water; season with pepper.

4 Set aside ¼ cup coconut milk for serving and add remaining coconut milk to saucepan.

5 Bring mixture to a boil; reduce heat, and simmer gently, stirring occasionally, until lentils are soft but not mushy, about 20 minutes. Season soup with more salt and pepper if needed.

6 To serve, divide soup among bowls. Drizzle with reserved coconut milk and top with cilantro. Serve with lime wedges to squeeze over the top.

SLOPPY JOES WITH LENTILS AND CHICKPEAS

These satisfying vegetarian sloppy joes are packed with plant-based protein from both lentils and chickpeas. Homemade BBQ sauce is so easy to make and so flavorful, you may never buy store-bought again!

TOTAL TIME: 30 minutes
SERVINGS: 6

INGREDIENTS

½ cup dry green lentils

1 (15 ounce) can cooked chickpeas, rinsed and drained (1.5 cups)

Coleslaw for topping, if desired

Whole grain or gluten free hamburger buns

BBQ SAUCE

1 teaspoon olive oil

1 small shallot, diced (about ¼ cup)

2 small cloves garlic, minced

1 cup tomato sauce

1 tablespoon ketchup

1 tablespoon pure maple syrup

2 teaspoons of apple cider vinegar

1 teaspoon tamari, liquid aminos or soy sauce

¾ teaspoon smoked paprika

½ teaspoon mustard powder

1 teaspoon chili powder

¼ teaspoon ground cumin

¼ teaspoon salt

⅛ teaspoon black pepper

INSTRUCTIONS

1 Place lentils in a medium-sized pot and cover with 1 cup of water and a pinch of salt. Bring to a boil, reduce to a simmer, and cook lentils until tender and cooked through, about 20 minutes.

2 Heat a large pan over medium heat and add olive oil and shallots. Season with a pinch of salt and cook for 2-3 minutes. Add garlic and cook for 1 more minute. Add tomato sauce, ketchup, maple syrup, apple cider vinegar, tamari, paprika, mustard powder, chili powder, cumin, salt, and pepper. Cook, stirring occasionally.

3 Add the cooked lentils and chickpeas to the BBQ sauce and cook for another few minutes until heated through.

4 Scoop the sloppy joe mix onto the buns and top with coleslaw, if desired.

EASY LENTIL MEATBALLS

Here is a healthier take on classic spaghetti and meatballs. Try these savory vegetarian meatballs served atop a whole grain, gluten-free pasta or veggie noodles like carrot, zucchini, or my favorite, spaghetti squash!

TOTAL TIME: 30 minutes
SERVINGS: 12 meatballs

INGREDIENTS

MEATBALLS

3 tablespoons + 1 teaspoon olive oil (divided)

1 medium shallot (minced)

3 cloves garlic (minced)

1 batch flax egg (1 tablespoons flaxseed meal + 2½ tablespoons water)

1 ½ cups cooked + cooled green lentils (cooked in vegetable stock)

1 ½ tablespoons dried Italian seasoning

¼ cup fresh Italian parsley

1 tablespoons tomato paste

5 - 6 tablespoons parmesan or vegan parmesan cheese (plus more for coating)

¼ teaspoon sea salt and black pepper, to taste

1 tablespoon coconut flour

FOR SERVING OPTIONAL

Whole grain pasta, gluten-free pasta, vegetable noodles (carrot, zucchini, spaghetti squash) and/ or marinara sauce

INSTRUCTIONS

1 Heat a large skillet over medium heat, preheat oven to 375 F, and line a baking sheet with parchment paper.

2 Once the skillet is hot, add 1 tablespoon olive oil, shallot, and garlic. Sauté for 2-3 minutes, or until slightly golden brown. Remove from heat and turn off the stove top.

3 In a food processor, add flaxseed and water and let set for 2-3 minutes.

4 Add cooked and cooled lentils, 1 teaspoon olive oil, sautéed garlic and shallot, Italian seasonings, parsley, tomato paste, vegan parmesan cheese, and a pinch each salt and pepper. Pulse, mixing until combined, but not puréed, leaving a little texture.

5 Taste and adjust seasonings as needed, adding more salt and pepper or herbs for flavor, add additional vegan parmesan if mixture is too moist, or a little olive oil to moisten if too dry. The texture should be dough-like.

6 Use a tablespoon or cookie dough scoop to scoop out rounded tablespoon amounts of dough and carefully form into balls. The mixture is moldable, but fragile, so the best way to do this is to rest the dough in the palm of one hand while using two fingers from the other hand to gently mold/form into a meatball. If it cracks, moisten your fingers with a little water to help reform/bind them. Repeat until all meatballs are formed—about 12.

7 Roll/coat each meatball in vegan parmesan cheese and arrange on a baking sheet.

8 Heat the skillet from earlier over medium heat. Once hot, add 1 tablespoon olive oil and half of the meatballs. Brown for 4-5 minutes, or until golden brown, shaking the pan or using a wooden spoon to roll the balls around to cook evenly on all sides.

9 As they are done cooking, transfer to your prepared baking sheet and set in the preheated oven. Repeat process, adding remaining 1 tablespoons olive oil to the skillet and sautéing remaining meatballs, then transfer to oven and bake for 10-15 minutes, while you prepare your carrot noodles, pasta and/or marinara sauce.

10 Remove meatballs from the oven and let cool slightly - they will firm up the longer they are cooled. Serve over pasta with marinara sauce.

VEGGIE, LENTIL AND POTATO FRITTERS

These yummy potato fritters with red lentils look and taste impressive, but they are easy to make. Delicious served with spicy Sriracha mayonnaise.

TOTAL TIME: 25 minutes
SERVINGS: 12 fritters

INGREDIENTS

FOR THE VEGETABLE POTATO FRITTERS:

¾ cup red lentils

1 small red onion, chopped

2 cloves of garlic, minced

2 medium-sized potatoes, raw and coarsely grated

1 medium-sized carrot, raw and coarsely grated

5 tablespoons all-purpose flour (gluten free if desired)

½ teaspoon smoked paprika powder

1 teaspoon paprika

1 teaspoon marjoram

Salt and black pepper, to taste

Olive oil or coconut oil for cooking in pan

FOR THE SRIRACHA MAYONNAISE:

3 tablespoons vegan mayonnaise

1 teaspoon tomato paste

1 teaspoon garlic powder

½ teaspoon smoked paprika powder

Salt and black pepper, to taste

Sriracha sauce, to taste

INSTRUCTIONS

1   Cook red lentils according to the instructions on the package.

2   In a large bowl, combine grated potatoes and carrots with cooked red lentils, garlic, onion, flour, and smoked paprika, paprika, marjoram, salt, and pepper, and stir well.

3   Heat the oil in a large pan, and add about 1½ heaped tablespoons for each fritter. Cook them on medium heat for three to four minutes on each side. Alternatively, you can also make them in the oven at 350 F degrees on parchment paper for an oil-free version (Bake for 20 minutes, flipping halfway).

4   For the vegan Sriracha mayonnaise, combine all ingredients and stir well.

5   Serve the fritters with a green salad topped with sriracha mayonnaise. Enjoy!

WALNUT TACOS WITH LIME CREAM SAUCE

These walnut meat tacos are a great alternative to beef, as they pack a protein punch and contain beneficial omega 3 fatty acids. Topped with tangy lime cream sauce, even walnut meat skeptics will enjoy this dish!

TOTAL TIME: 10 minutes
SERVINGS: 6 tacos

INGREDIENTS

WALNUT TACOS

1.5 cups de-shelled raw walnuts

1 teaspoon garlic powder

½ teaspoon cumin

½ teaspoon chili powder

1 tablespoon tamari, soy sauce or coconut aminos

6 taco shells (I prefer organic & gluten-free)

TOPPINGS

1 cup carrots, chopped

1 cup red cabbage, chopped

¼ - ½ cup onion chopped

Cilantro, chopped

Hot sauce

LIME CASHEW SOUR CREAM

1 cup cashews, soaked overnight (or soaked at least 10 minutes in boiling water)

⅓ - ½ cup water (and more if needed)

2 tablespoons lime juice

1 tablespoon apple cider vinegar

Pinch of salt

INSTRUCTIONS

1 Add walnuts to a food processor and pulse to process until mixture is kind of "meaty."

2 Transfer processed walnuts to a bowl and add garlic powder, cumin, chili powder, and tamari. Mix well to combine. Salt and pepper to taste. Set aside.

3 To make the lime cashew sour cream: Blend all ingredients on a high-speed until smooth. Add more water if needed to achieve a sour cream consistency. If too thin, add additional cashews.

4 To serve: Fill taco shells with walnut mixture and add toppings of choice.

5 Garnish tacos with lime cashew sour cream and enjoy!

VEGAN "TUNA" SALAD WITH SUNFLOWER SEEDS

Lunch time just got tastier with this vegan take on a deli classic. This healthy "tuna" salad uses soaked sunflower seeds as a substitute for the tuna and for the mayo! Lemon, dill, and Dijon make this salad pop with flavor. Serve over a salad or in a wrap.

TOTAL TIME: 15 minutes (plus optional soaking time)
SERVINGS: 4

INGREDIENTS

1 cup raw hulled sunflower seeds

Juice of ½ lemon (about 2 tablespoons)

2 teaspoons Dijon mustard

Kosher salt

2 tablespoons fresh dill, coarsely chopped

2 tablespoons parsley leaves, coarsely chopped

¼ teaspoon paprika

1 stalk celery with leaves, chopped

1 small shallot, chopped

Freshly ground black pepper

SERVING SUGGESTIONS:

Whole wheat wraps with lettuce, tomato, and avocado

INSTRUCTIONS

1   Cover the sunflower seeds with at least ¼ inch of water and soak at room temperature in an airtight container for at least 24 hours. The seeds are ready when they have nearly doubled in size.

2   Drain the seeds and pulse half (about 1 cup) with the lemon juice, mustard and ¼ teaspoon salt in a food processor until almost smooth, scraping down the bowl as needed.

3   Add the remaining seeds, along with the dill, parsley, paprika, celery, shallot, ¼ teaspoon salt and a few grinds of pepper to the food processor. Pulse until the mixture resembles tuna salad. Refrigerate in an airtight container for up to 3 days.

4   Serve over greens or fill a whole wheat or gluten free wrap vegan "tuna" salad and your favorite fixings like with lettuce, tomato, avocado, or shredded carrots.

PORTOBELLO "STEAKS"

Satisfy your steak cravings with flavorful portobello mushrooms. These juicy mushroom "steaks" are a delicious plant-based alternative to meat.

TOTAL TIME: 30 minutes
SERVINGS: 4

INGREDIENTS

4 large portobello mushrooms, de-stemmed

¼ cup olive oil

2 tablespoons balsamic vinegar

2 tablespoons steak seasoning, salt-free

INSTRUCTIONS

1   Preheat the oven to 400 F.

2   In a large shallow dish, combine olive oil, balsamic vinegar, and steak spice. With a pastry brush, generously brush the marinade on the tops and bottoms of each mushroom.

3   Place mushrooms in the remaining marinade, top side down and bake, uncovered, for 20 minutes. Remove from the oven, flip, and bake another 5-10 minutes until mushrooms are fully cooked.

4   Serve with roasted potatoes and grilled vegetables.

VEGAN PUMPKIN SOUP

This vegan pumpkin soup recipe with minimal ingredients is easy to make using one pot and ready in 30 minutes! This healthy soup features red lentils and is creamy without the cream!

TOTAL TIME: 30 minutes
SERVINGS: 4-6

INGREDIENTS

1 tablespoon olive oil

1 large yellow onion, diced

4 - 6 cloves garlic, minced

1 - 2 teaspoons fresh thyme, chopped

Pinch of red pepper flakes

4 - 5-pound baking pumpkin, peeled, seeds removed, cubed

1 cup dried red lentils

6 cups broth or water

Salt and pepper, to taste

¼ cup chopped parsley, to garnish

Toasted pumpkin seeds (pepitas) to garnish

INSTRUCTIONS

1 In a large pot, heat olive oil over medium heat, add onion and garlic, and sauté for 5 minutes until slightly browned.

2 Add thyme, red pepper flakes, salt, and pepper. Stir and cook 1 minute more until fragrant.

3 Add pumpkin, red lentils and broth. Bring to a boil, then cover. Reduce to low and simmer at a gentle boil for 20 minutes.

4 Simmer until pumpkin is fork tender and lentils are soft.

5 Remove soup from heat and let cool a few minutes. Using an immersion blender (or stand blender), puree the soup to desired consistency. Salt and pepper to taste.

6 Garnish with fresh parsley and toasted pumpkin seeds.

WEST AFRICAN PEANUT STEW

West African Peanut Stew is one of my favorite dishes. This warming, hearty stew is creamy and delicious. For those with peanut allergy, almond butter can be substituted. Traditionally this is a spicy stew, but by simply reducing or omitting the jalapenos, you can adjust the heat to your taste.

TOTAL TIME: 30 minutes
SERVINGS: 4-6

INGREDIENTS

1 tablespoon olive oil

1 large yellow onion, diced

5 - 6 cloves garlic, minced

2 - 3 tablespoons ginger, grated

1 tablespoon ground coriander

1 - 2 jalapeno peppers,
seeded and diced

2 - 3 pounds sweet potatoes,
peeled and cut into ½ inch cubes

1 can (15-ounce) diced tomatoes,
with juices

4 cups vegetable broth or water
(or combo)

¾ cup natural peanut butter
(creamy or smooth)

5 ounces fresh spinach, chopped
or baby spinach

2 lemons, juiced

Salt & pepper, to taste

GARNISH:

Fresh cilantro, chopped

Peanuts, crushed or whole

Dash of hot sauce like Sriracha
or tabasco, optional

Serve over grain of choice (rice,
quinoa or couscous), optional

INSTRUCTIONS

1   In a large pot, heat oil over medium heat, add the onion, garlic, ginger, and chili peppers if using, and sauté for 5 minutes, stirring frequently.

2   Add the sweet potatoes, tomatoes, garlic, ginger, coriander, tomatoes with juices, and broth. Bring to a boil. Reduce heat and simmer covered for 15 minutes, or until sweet potatoes are fork tender.

3   Turn off heat and add peanut butter and lemon juice. Stir well to combine. Add spinach, stir until wilted.

4   Soup will thicken upon cooling. Season with salt and pepper to taste.

5   Serve over a grain or as a stew with optional garnishes such as cilantro, chopped peanuts, hot sauce.

QUICK AND EASY BROCCOLI WITH GARLIC SAUCE

Broccoli with garlic sauce is spicy, sweet, and delicious! The sesame seeds provide a satisfying crunch. Serve over rice for a main dish or as a tasty vegetable side.

TOTAL TIME: 20 minutes
SERVINGS: 4

INGREDIENTS

1 tablespoon olive oil

6 cups fresh broccoli florets

2 teaspoons cornstarch

1 - 2 tablespoons sesame seeds, for garnish

SAUCE INGREDIENTS

½ cup vegetable broth or water

2 tablespoons coconut aminos, soy sauce, or tamari

2 tablespoons maple syrup or honey

1 tablespoon sesame oil

3 cloves garlic, minced

1 - 2 teaspoons red pepper flakes

INSTRUCTIONS

1 In a large measuring cup, mix broth, coconut aminos, maple syrup, sesame oil, garlic, and red pepper flakes together.

2 Heat olive oil in a wok or large sauté pan over medium-high heat on the stovetop.

3 Once the oil is hot, add the broccoli and sauté until florets start to soften, about 3 to 5 minutes

4 Add all but 2 tablespoons of the sauce to the broccoli. Then stir the cornstarch into the remaining 2 tablespoons of leftover sauce and whisk until there are no lumps.

5 Add remaining cornstarch and sauce mixture to the broccoli and cook until the sauce thickens, about 3 to 5 minutes, stirring frequently.

6 Remove from heat, add sesame seeds, stir to combine, and enjoy!

HONEY ROASTED CARROTS

Honey roasted carrots are a scrumptious side dish for any meal. For a vegan option, feel free to substitute 100% maple syrup.

TOTAL TIME: 50 minutes
SERVINGS: 8

INGREDIENTS

2 pounds carrots, peeled

1 tablespoon olive oil

1 tablespoon coconut oil, melted

½ - 1 teaspoon salt

1 tablespoon honey
(or maple syrup)

INSTRUCTIONS

1 Preheat oven to 425 F. Lightly grease a large baking pan.

2 Cut carrots into the shape and size of your choosing.

3 In a small bowl, mix together olive oil and melted coconut oil.

4 Put carrots in a large mixing bowl and toss with the olive oil/coconut oil mixture and salt until all the carrots are evenly coated.

5 Spread carrots in a single layer on the prepared baking sheet and roast in the preheated oven for 15 minutes.

6 Shake the pan to stir and roast 10 additional minutes, or until carrots are just starting to brown.

7 Remove the carrots from the oven and drizzle with honey or maple syrup, then shake the pan until the honey or maple syrup is evenly distributed.

8 Return the carrots to the oven and roast for an additional 10-15 minutes or until carrots are just golden-brown!

9 Best served immediately. Enjoy!

CRISPY ZUCCHINI FRITTERS

Move over French fries... these tasty fritters are not only oil-free, but baked, not fried! They're simply delicious topped with a tangy lemon cashew sauce. Any leftover sauce can be used as a flavorful homemade salad dressing.

TOTAL TIME: 55 minutes
SERVINGS: 3-4

INGREDIENTS

2 small zucchinis, shredded and excess water squeezed out

⅔ cup corn kernels (frozen corn defrosted is fine)

3 tablespoons creamy almond butter

½ cup gluten-free oat flour

2 teaspoons garlic powder

2 teaspoons onion powder

¾ teaspoon fine sea salt

¼ teaspoon ground black pepper

1 teaspoon smoked paprika

CREAMY LEMON PEPPER SAUCE

½ heaping cup raw cashews (cooked in boiling water for 10 minutes, and drained or simply soak cashews in cold water overnight and drain.)

2 tablespoons fresh lemon juice

6 - 8 tablespoons water

¼ teaspoon onion powder

¼ teaspoon garlic powder

¼ teaspoon ground black pepper

¼ teaspoon fine sea salt

INSTRUCTIONS

1 Preheat the oven to 400 F and line a baking pan with parchment paper.

2 Shred zucchini using the larger holes on your grater to form long strips. After shredding, loosely measure 2 ½ cups.

3 Place your shredded zucchini into a strainer and place a couple of paper towels on top and press firmly to squeeze out excess water. Place the dried zucchini into a large bowl.

4 Add the corn and almond butter.

5 In a separate small bowl, combine the oat flour, onion powder, garlic powder, salt, pepper and smoked paprika and stir until well mixed.

6 Add the dry mixture to the zucchini mixture and stir for a good couple of minutes until it all comes together. It will seem too dry at first, but keep stirring and pressing the batter with the back of the spoon and it will start to stick. It should be moist and somewhat sticky.

7 Divide into 4 sections and form balls and then flatten out into little patties about ½ inch thick. Place onto parchment paper and (optionally) chill in the fridge for 30 minutes to firm.

8 Bake the patties for 25 minutes, carefully flip them over with a spatula (they will be tender but should flip easily) and bake for another 10-15 minutes depending on how crispy you want them. They should be a very golden brown color. Let cool for about 10 minutes before serving.

9 While fritters are baking, prepare the creamy lemon pepper sauce.

10 Cool, serve with sauce, and enjoy!

CREAMY CASHEW LEMON PEPPER SAUCE:

1 Add the soaked and drained cashews, lemon juice, water, garlic powder, onion powder, pepper and salt to a blender. Blend until completely smooth. You will need to scrape the sides a few times during blending.

2 Taste and adjust spices if necessary. The sauce will thicken the longer it sits and especially after being stored in the fridge. Simply thin with a small amount of water as needed to achieve desired consistency.

LEMON POPPY SEED MUFFINS

These gluten-free muffins are tangy and light! Lemon juice and lemon zest combine well with the crunchy poppy seeds to make a tangy, sweet treat for a light breakfast or snack.

TOTAL TIME: 35 minutes
SERVINGS: 12 muffins

INGREDIENTS

FOR THE MUFFINS:

¼ cup coconut oil (or olive or vegetable oil)

4/5 cup unsweetened almond milk (or other plant-based milk)

6 tablespoons lemon juice

2 tablespoons lemon zest (use unwaxed lemons)

10 tablespoons maple syrup

1 teaspoon vanilla extract

Pinch salt

3 tablespoons poppy seeds

1 ¼ cup almond meal

1 ¼ cup gluten-free flour blend (or pastry flour if not gluten-free)

2 heaped teaspoons baking powder

¼ teaspoon baking soda

FOR THE SYRUP (OPTIONAL):

2 tablespoons lemon juice

4 tablespoons maple syrup

INSTRUCTIONS

FOR THE MUFFINS:

1 Preheat oven to 350 F.

2 Place the coconut oil in a large bowl and melt over a saucepan of boiling water or in the microwave.

3 Once oil is melted, add the milk, lemon juice, lemon zest, maple syrup, vanilla, salt, poppy seeds, and almond meal.

4 Sift in the flour, baking powder, and baking soda.

5 Mix well, adding a tiny splash more milk if it's looking too dry.

6 Fill muffin liners or well-oiled muffin pan with batter about halfway.

7 Bake for 15-20 minutes until risen and an inserted knife comes out clean.

FOR THE SYRUP:

1 While the muffins are baking, mix together the lemon juice and maple syrup.

2 Drizzle over the muffins as soon as they are taken out of the oven to allow the syrup to soak into the muffins.

CRISPY CRUNCHY ROASTED CHICKPEAS

Roasted chickpeas are a favorite snack in our household. The secret to getting them extra crispy is to dry roast them first, and then add the seasonings for the last few minutes of cooking time. This is an easy to make, vegan, antiinflammatory snack that everyone will love.

TOTAL TIME: 35 minutes
SERVINGS: 2

INGREDIENTS

1 (19-ounce) can chickpeas, drained and rinsed

1 tablespoon olive oil

½ teaspoon garlic powder

½ teaspoon ginger powder

½ teaspoon turmeric powder

¼ teaspoon paprika

½ teaspoon salt

INSTRUCTIONS

1 Preheat oven to 375 F.

2 Spread chickpeas in a single layer on a baking sheet. It's okay if they are still a bit wet, they will dry out in the oven. Bake for 20-25 minutes, stopping to shake the pan every now and then. *Make sure you do shake the pan once or twice when the chickpeas are baking, this helps them dry out properly and get crispy.

3 Remove chickpeas from the oven and carefully add the hot chickpeas to a bowl along with the olive oil, garlic, ginger, turmeric, paprika, and salt. Toss well to coat the chickpeas evenly. Spread the seasoned chickpeas back onto the baking sheet and return to the oven for another 10 to 15 minutes until they are golden and crispy.

4 Remove from the oven and let cool a bit before enjoying.

SALTED CARAMEL COCONUT BLISS BALLS

These grab and go salted caramel bliss balls are a decadent, guilt-free indulgence! With only 5 wholesome ingredients, they are an easy to make, healthy treat to enjoy on the go.

TOTAL TIME: 15 minutes
SERVINGS: 12 Bliss Balls

INGREDIENTS

1 cup pitted Medjool dates (packed)

1 cup almonds

¼ cup unsweetened shredded coconut (plus extra for rolling)

¼ teaspoon vanilla extract

¼ teaspoon salt

INSTRUCTIONS

1 Add Medjool dates, almonds, shredded coconut, vanilla extract and salt to a food processor and pulse until it forms into a sticky dough.

2 Using your hands, roll into bite-sized balls, and then roll into a plate of shredded coconut to coat if desired.

3 Store in the fridge in an airtight container.

HOMEMADE TRAIL MIX

Homemade trail mix is a great alternative to store-bought trail mix, because you can customize it to your taste. My favorite blend is raw walnuts, pecans, pumpkin seeds, sunflower seeds, dried cherries, crystallized ginger, and of course... chocolate chips! I like to keep a stash in my backpack while hiking, and at the office for a quick, healthy pick-me-up when hunger hits.

TOTAL TIME: 5 minutes
SERVINGS: 4

INGREDIENTS

½ cup raw or dry roasted nuts
of choice (walnuts, almonds,
pecans, pistachios, cashews,
etc.)

½ cup raw or dry roasted seeds
of choice (pumpkin seeds,
sunflower seeds, etc.)

½ cup unsweetened dried fruit
of choice (raisins, cranberries,
cherries, etc.)

½ cup chocolate chips or chunks

⅛ cup crystallized ginger, diced
(optional)

INSTRUCTIONS

1   Add all ingredients into a
    bowl and mix together until
    evenly combined.

2   Place ½ cup of trail mix into
    4 separate portable storage
    bags or sealed containers.
    Store on the counter or in a
    cupboard for up to 1 month.
    Enjoy!

GREEN PEA DIP

Here is a fresh take on a traditional dip. Sweet peas (fresh or frozen!) make this bright green, tangy hummus one of my favorite party appetizers to share. Aquafaba (the reserved liquid from canned chickpeas) makes the texture smooth and creamy.

TOTAL TIME: 5 minutes
SERVINGS: 10

INGREDIENTS

15-ounce can of chickpeas, not yet drained

1 cup fresh or frozen peas

2 tablespoons tahini

2 teaspoons lemon juice

1 clove of garlic minced

Pinch of salt and pepper

INSTRUCTIONS

1 Drain the chickpeas over a bowl to collect the liquid (this is called by the fancy name, aquafaba), then add the chickpeas to a blender or food processor.

2 Defrost frozen peas under hot water to thaw, then add to the blender, with tahini, lemon juice, garlic salt and pepper as well as 4 tablespoons of the aquafaba.

3 Blend for a few minutes until thick and creamy. You may need to scrape the sides down periodically. Add a little more aquafaba if necessary to achieve a thick and creamy consistency.

4 Delicious served with carrot sticks, celery, cucumber, sugar snap peas, or pita chips.

CHOCOLATE BANANA SMOOTHIE

Start your day right with this satisfying vegan dark chocolate banana smoothie. This creamy, delicious shake is high in fiber, omega 3 fatty acids, protein, and a variety of vitamins and minerals.

TOTAL TIME: 10 minutes
SERVINGS: 1

INGREDIENTS

1 frozen banana

2 tablespoons raw cacao powder

1 tablespoon chia seeds

1 tablespoon ground flax

Handful of greens such as baby spinach or kale

½ teaspoon sea salt

1 serving vegan vanilla protein powder

1 ½ cups unsweetened almond milk, soy, coconut, rice, hemp

Pinch of cinnamon

INSTRUCTIONS

1 Add all ingredients to a high-speed blender and blend on max for 30-60 seconds until completely smooth and creamy.

2 Pour into a glass and enjoy!

EASY HOMEMADE 5-SEED CRACKERS

Looking for a way to add seeds to your diet like sunflower, pumpkin, chia, sesame, and flax? These easy to make, home-made crackers are a great way to incorporate more healthy fats, plant-based protein, fiber, magnesium, and antioxidants into a delicious snack!

TOTAL TIME: 1 hour
SERVINGS: 10

INGREDIENTS

1 cup sunflower seeds

¾ cup pumpkin seeds

½ cup chia seeds

½ cup sesame seeds, (I used a mix of black and white sesame seeds)

¼ cup flax seeds

1 teaspoon salt

1 ½ cups water

1 tablespoon dried herbs of your choice (thyme, oregano, garlic, rosemary)

1 teaspoon chili flakes, (optional)

INSTRUCTIONS

1 Preheat oven to 350 F. Line 2 baking sheets with parchment paper.

2 In a large bowl, mix all ingredients together and leave to soak for 10-15 minutes until water is absorbed by the seeds.

3 Stir briskly and then split the mixture over two lined baking trays and spread evenly into a layer about 3-4 mm thick.

4 Bake for about one hour (switching the trays around halfway through), or until nicely golden brown and crisp.

5 Remove from the oven, allow to cool, then break into irregular pieces. Store in an airtight container. Enjoy served with hummus, guacamole or bean dip.

BAKED KALE CHIPS

I love kale chips! Like potato chips, you cannot stop at just eating one! This homemade version is much less expensive than the store bought varieties and easy to make. Low calorie, nutritious, and certainly delicious. Great for parties!

TOTAL TIME: 20 minutes
SERVINGS: 2-4

INGREDIENTS

1 bunch fresh kale

1 teaspoon sea salt or seasoned salt

3 tablespoons olive oil

INSTRUCTIONS

1 Preheat an oven to 350F. Line a cookie sheet with parchment paper.

2 With a knife or kitchen shears carefully remove the leaves from the thick stems and tear into bite size pieces. Wash and **thoroughly** dry kale with a salad spinner or blotting well with a paper towel.

3 Drizzle kale with olive oil and sprinkle with sea salt or seasoning salt. Toss to coat evenly.

4 Bake until the edges brown but are not burnt, 10 to 15 minutes. Cool and enjoy!

NO-BAKE GRANOLA BARS

Soft, chewy home-made granola bars taste so much better than store-bought. And you can customize to your taste! No artificial ingredients or refined sugar in this recipe. Create your own healthy on-the-go snack by combining your favorite tahini or nut butter with maple syrup, oats, dried fruits, and seeds.

TOTAL TIME: 10 minutes
SERVINGS: 8

INGREDIENTS

1 cup tahini (or substitute smooth peanut, almond or sunflower butter)

½ cup 100% maple syrup

2 ½ cups gluten free rolled oats

¼-½ cup dried fruits and seeds (I like pumpkin, raw sunflower seeds and dried cherries)

2-3 tablespoons of mini chocolate chips (dairy free if vegan), optional

INSTRUCTIONS

1 Line an 8 x 8-inch pan with parchment paper and set aside.

2 On the stovetop, combine your tahini and maple syrup in a large pot and heat until warm and well combined. Stir well.

3 Remove from heat and add rolled oats. Mix until combined. Fold in dried fruits and seeds and mix very well, until fully incorporated. Add chocolate chips if using.

4 Transfer granola bar batter into the lined pan and press firmly into place.

5 Refrigerate for at least an hour, until the bars are firm. Cut into 16 small bars or 8 large ones. Enjoy!

SPINACH & ARTICHOKE WHITE BEAN DIP

This creamy spinach and artichoke white bean dip is a perfect appetizer or side dish. Scoop it up with raw veggies, pita chips, or crackers, or spread it on your favorite crusty bread.

TOTAL TIME: 30 minutes
SERVINGS: makes 3 cups

INGREDIENTS

¼ cup bread crumbs
(gluten-free if preferred)

2 tablespoons olive oil, divided

1 large shallot or medium onion,
diced

3 garlic cloves, minced, or
½ teaspoon garlic powder

1 can (14-ounce) artichoke
hearts in water, drained and
chopped

5 ounces baby spinach or
1 bunch spinach, roughly
chopped

1 can (15-ounce) cannellini, navy
or great northern beans, drained
and rinsed

1 lemon, juiced

¼ cup water

2 - 3 tablespoons nutritional
yeast, optional

1 teaspoon dried thyme

Salt and pepper to taste

¼ - ½ teaspoon of red
pepper flakes

INSTRUCTIONS

1   Preheat oven to 375 F.

2   In a small bowl combine the bread crumbs with 1 tablespoon olive oil, mix well, set aside.

3   Heat the remaining oil in a skillet/pan over medium heat, add onions and sauté for about 5 minutes, until onions are translucent. Add in garlic and cook 1 minute, add artichoke hearts and spinach, cook until spinach wilts.

4   In a food processor, add beans, lemon juice, water, nutritional yeast, thyme, salt, pepper and red pepper flakes. Process until creamy, scraping down the sides as needed.

5   Add the puree to the sautéed artichoke and spinach mixture and mix well.

6   Transfer the mixture to an oiled baking dish. Top the mixture with a layer of olive oil bread crumbs and bake, covered for 10 minutes. After 10 minutes, remove cover and cook an additional 10 minutes. Place under broiler for 1-2 minutes to achieve golden brown topping. Be mindful to avoid burning.

7   Serve warm as a dip with veggies, pita chips or crackers. You can also serve this as a delicious spread with a crusty bread of your choice.